GNOSIS

A PHILOSOPHICAL PSYCHOLOGY CONCERNING THE EMERGENCE OF INDIVIDUATED HOLISTIC INTELLIGENCE

S. R. ALLEN

Copyright 2012
All Rights Reserved

ISBN's:
978-0-9887067-2-9 Hardcover
978-0-9887067-1-2 Paperback
978-0-9887067-0-5 e-book

U.S. Copyright Office registration number:
Txu 1-830-305
Allen, S. R.
Gnosis A Philosophical Psychology Concerning the Emergence of Individuated Holistic Intelligence
English. 2012

GNOSTIKO LLP
PUBLISHING

Contents

PREFACE

This book is the result of a long and systematic course of research and a line of questioning in an attempt to understand and convey essential ideas concerning the real circumstances of life and living in a less than hospitable world. My goal has been to clearly articulate the significance of several important facts which have been generally overlooked by our so-called "modern" traditions of psychology, philosophy, science, and religion. Although the book is somewhat terse and to the point, it is not without a wealth of substantiating detail. More details will be found within the mind of the reader himself/herself while thinking through the book. It should be read and re-read several times over a period of time, not only to refresh the memory about what it reveals, but also as a reminder and to shed more light on how the statements in it correlate with the reader's own experiences in advancements in thinking capacity, reasoning, and insight.

There are various subtle processes continually operating in the individual mind not usually detected or understood. As we become more and more aware of these, many of life's conflicts and frustrations are revealed in their hidden simplicity and the solutions to all kinds of problems can be suddenly, obviously known.

The book is purposefully compact and dense, serving as a short but powerful stroke that can cut the root of a large, poisonous weed, doing away with the source of the poison itself, instead of engaging in extensive plucking at the various parts of the weed itself in hopes of keeping it manageable by continual pruning.

The book is structured in a very linear fashion, building an idea pattern based on a problem and a solution to it. Within the analytical part of the book there is a progressive dialectic revealing how errant reasoning develops slowly into blatant delusion. The next step in delusional thinking produces motivations that become the hidden aspects of nearly everyone's problems.

The last chapter shows explicitly how to win the victory over the hidden problem and incorporates the best of both Eastern and Western esoteric formulas for profound meditative and contemplative practices.

_____The Author

CHAPTER ONE
THE PROBLEM

Gnosis: Knowledge; to know. Gnosis is sophisticated and profound knowledge of spiritual subjects, especially those subjects that are esoteric, secret, hidden, or difficult to comprehend. Gnosis is a special revealing knowledge intended only for the competent few or an inner group capable of understanding abstract or complicated concepts. Gnosis is a superior understanding that transcends even the most developed rational capacity, and is accessible only through individual illumination.

Deep within the conscious being of every individual there is an insatiable longing to know, to discover (or perhaps to rediscover) the unknown, to excavate the depths of memory and the subconscious with the hope that hidden therein may lie the forgotten knowledge concerning existence and destiny. If this kind of knowledge was obtainable, then more competence and skill could be developed for the pursuit of a richer life and a better destiny.

1

Throughout known human history this insatiable longing has motivated all serious investigations concerned with the perennial questions of philosophy and science, and the often obsessive entanglement with the ideas of religions.

If we are to consider ourselves as credible persons, we cannot create or re-create any humbug of a "spiritual philosophy" or theoretical ideology. That destroys the creativity of the "spirit". We must go forth to penetrate the total individual and collective psyche; to create and sustain a freedom of enquiry toward the ultimate that a human being can possibly achieve – enlightenment. We cannot justifiably pursue a motivation to confine anyone's intelligence in a format of dogma or theory; we must free our intelligence from all such imprisonments. We must free our consciousness, first at the individual level and then move to help other sentient beings to desire and accomplish this freedom.

This is a difficult task awaiting anyone who may be in the pursuit of a better existence and destiny. There must be found an answer to the "purpose of life", what this purpose really is, or even if there is a purpose. If there is a definite purpose then anyone who comes into harmony with the general purpose of existence will automatically transcend most of what is unwanted in life or hard to deal with. How to think and how to act in harmony with existential purpose is knowing what to do and avoid doing. It is impossible for anyone to proclaim truly that they know what they are doing unless they understand the purpose of existence. Most people think they know what they are doing, but it is only a surface recognition, not any sort of insight into the reality of things. What is really relevant is knowing what to do and avoid doing in a context of harmonious accord with the real purpose of Being itself. To be out of harmony with what's really going on is to invite discord which will result in turmoil and conflict. Perhaps these kinds of problems are needed in order to activate the motivation for development of reason in the individual's thinking. The existence of the universe apparently provides for this, and we will explore this further on.

The operations of the phenomenal realm of nature, when these structures and patterns are conscientiously investigated, indicate an inherent intelligence within the order of things and events we observe. Data from both past and present science, philosophy, and religion seem to wantonly bypass or ignore the implications of pattern and the indications of intelligent order and operation in nature. Such data in its partiality supports commonly held theories, beliefs, and dogmas which tend to disregard the crucial importance of finding true and complete answers to the most important questions. Because of the persistent hard fact that humankind still has no definitive, conclusive answers to these questions of origin, existence, or purpose, it must be admitted that the human race is yet encumbered with ignorance. It is ignorance that inevitably results in all problems, afflictions, and conflicts of life, and the honest recognition of ignorance is the central valid basis from which a potentially productive search must proceed. The acknowledgment of ignorance is the first evidence of possible emergence from it and from its effects.

We know about the many characteristics of things and their many details, but we, as conditioned selves identified as body-mind objects perceiving other objects, cannot sensually experience any thing or know just what any thing is really, or what any event is really – in itself. Through the dialectical consideration of our lack of total knowledge of any one thing, we can know one thing – ignorance. Ignorance is an absence of knowledge and not something we can actually think about clearly. But we can know what ignorance is, directly and intuitively, as that which is prior to knowledge. We cannot seek to know or to inspect existence or Being in the conventional way of getting knowledge because existence cannot be inspected from a viewpoint outside of existence. Likewise, consciousness cannot be inspected from a prior or separate position. Consideration and contemplation of such things helps to relax the aberrant mind from its chronic dualistic conceptualizations and enables us to bypass dualistic thinking for just an instant, so to get a glimpse of another way of "seeing".

The wall of ignorance is not insurmountable, and once beyond it we will enter into the light of Gnosis. Ignorance obscures the perception of the reality of things and situations just like a wall is impossible to see through. Even if a small hole is put in the wall, vision will be severely restricted and most of what is on the other side will still remain hidden and unknown. When ignorance remains in the mind, then everything associated with ignorance can be expected to arise. What we don't know can hurt us, but when ignorance is absent the potential for what is hurtful is also absent and herein lies the beginning of intelligent search for real answers to meaningful questions. But almost everyone already realizes this, more or less, so what we need to investigate into is just what it is that keeps us in our ignorance, and this is not generally realized.

Human perceptual capacities are obviously inefficient and lacking clarity. Problems which perpetually remain unsolved are the unceasing evidence of undeveloped and deficient reason and clear thinking. Unclear thinking based on incomplete or partial data produces only speculation and conjecture, and all such theoretical presumptions are in some degree faulty, making them sometimes worse than useless. Speculation based on incomplete or errant evidence always clouds judgement and reason. Since our physical senses are limited to the observation of the phenomenal realm of objectivity, any attempt to rely on the limited arena of the physical senses for conducting a complete investigation of the inner realms of mind and life will prove to be folly. Scientific evidence that has resulted from intelligent and detailed research and analysis can be useful, but only if well-scrutinized and properly regarded.

Reason is a necessity in the analytical integration of facts and evidence when engaging in a determined search for truth, so superior knowledge will be attained only by those who have transcended the effects of ignorance and developed good reasoning abilities, thus overcoming the defects of sense-perception and intelligence. Problems within conditioned life experience emerge as the results of undeveloped thinking capacity and can never be solved or eradicated until the faults in thinking and reasoning are recognized and corrected. It's a paradoxical situation: ignorance is incapable of recognizing ignorance. The great majority of people are functioning not only under the limitations of underdeveloped and immature perceptual faculties, but also under the effects of some degree of mental aberration such as wrong knowledge, superstition, anxiety, the ego-notion, and a host of inadequacies and accumulated negative tendencies that inevitably create the discomforts and stresses of physical, emotional, and mental afflictions and conflicts.

As human beings we are compelled to live our lives in a procession of an almost endless series of experiences. Usually we do not have a very developed understanding of how each experience is connected with the previous conditions that create the flow of situations and events. Whatever we can conjure up in our minds about what these experiences really mean in the context of our definable state of being is of little worth unless it is based in fact instead of wishful thinking. Wishful thinking usually conforms to fixed formulations of ideas handed down from generation to generation and from culture to culture. It is just these fixed forms that we have to learn to avoid when we process new information; our tendency is to add new facts or ideas onto an already well-structured dogma or theory. This has been going on for ages with little or no progress toward answering ultimate questions, and the consequence is that people are still uncomfortable, incomplete, and still longing to know that unknown something that might give them ultimate fulfilment.

One may seek for some sort of fundamental happiness, contentment, or satisfaction in life, but not finding this object of the search, one then realizes only the perpetual dissatisfaction and subconscious anxieties that are the substratum of most motives. There is an absence of knowledge in the faith-based religions and an absence of analysis of the dilemma people seem to be always entangled within. Most religions are concerned with the promulgation of their particular dogmas and not with analysis and discovery of what is at the root of dilemma and anxiety. People congregate around the axis of a dogmatic belief; the wheel of the congregation becomes a feedback loop of escapisms – subhuman games promoted by a church or organization which appeal to a neurotic and naive majority. This majority, the congregation, then becomes more and more enmeshed in group-actuated feelings of hope and certainty to escape from fear and uncertainty – and death. The followers exorcize themselves from the development and use of their rational powers, and thus the religion becomes a diluted and childish pursuit of imbalanced action and thought – an irresponsible cult of superstition and self-interests.

The average individual cannot relax, cannot enter into a personal quietude. He is almost constantly distracted in some degree, and obsessively entangled in daydream. Seeking some form of contentment or happiness through collecting possessions is the most prominent materialistic expression of goal-seeking. But the contentment or happiness people presume themselves to be seeking is usually always diminished, negated, or destroyed by the consequent cares and worries that accompany the search. The ceaseless craving to attain more and more possessions supposedly necessary for being happy is the very poison that pollutes the possibility for happiness. Some people do become clever enough to gain possession of some of the (presumed) needed items that must be gained to achieve the (presumed) goal such as money, a great name, power, fame, prestige, but their happiness and contentment are marred or cancelled out by the fear of losing these possessions and the exhausting struggle to maintain them.

Most people cannot relax because their discomfort is too prominent; they are ill at ease and unfulfilled, perhaps even with a subtle sense of impending doom – or at least some little perplexing trouble or anxiety about something not quite right. There is a lack of knowledge about what it is that may be wrong or what it is that is in the background creating dis-ease, an unidentified psychological complaint perhaps, or a feeling of insecurity or vulnerability. In order to escape from this type of feeling, people are motivated to pursue some form of distraction away from it, usually in the common manner of entertainment or absorption in trivial activities. Some seek the escape from the feelings of insecurity by adopting the tenets and beliefs of some form of religion. Through the dogmatic belief systems of theistic religions designed for mass consumption people seek to free themselves from the pernicious feelings of insecurity, anxiety, and frustration. It is usually not the "morality of righteousness" that is motivating such seekers, but the feelings of relief they sometimes experience when accepting some concept of "salvation". Everyone knows they will die, lose everything they have accumulated, and end a state of life, the only state they have real experience in, and enter into a questionable state of which they have no experience or real knowledge – death – a completely helpless state.

This kind of anxiety makes the daily situations of life sometimes nearly unendurable, and without entertainments and distractions life can become full of suppressed fearfulness. The power of most faith-based religion depends on this kind of psychological fear for the promulgation and survival of the dogma it presents as a solution to counter the fear and anxiety of the faith-holders. Thus, a hope/fear psychological neurosis becomes the playing field upon which the dramas of hive-mentality are enacted by the deluded majority of unquestioning people. Most people live in a mode of tolerance, a tolerance of suppressed anxieties. Supposing that most of the other people they know, or know of, actually know what they are doing, understand reality, and are acting accordingly, most individuals automatically follow along with the collective social, political, or religious paradigm, struggling always to fit in, to conform, and to reap the benefits of so doing. Everything seems good enough as long as the unanswered questions and the fears remain suppressed, so there gets to be a heavy investment in the continual distractions and pseudo-security the social and religio-political systems seem to offer. People get to be like the proverbial ostrich with its head buried in the sand. But from time to time events occur which expose pent-up anxieties; friends become enemies, loved ones become hated ones, and everybody ends up getting old and dying. The collections of possessions finally obsess and then possess their possessor. Everything is always disappearing, changing, changing. The search for security, consolation, and contentment though is endless; from the womb until the tomb uncertainty reigns. The unreal becomes dominant in the minds of the unwary, and they succumb to its influence in the refusal of the real.

The never-ending search for stimulation and entertainment is an escapist tactic which can become an obsessive habitual attempt to suppress the oppressiveness of the trivialities of a bewildered life. External excitation becomes the formula for dealing with the lack of richness in inner life, but these sorts of compensation formulas are always only a temporary diversion and self-defeating in the long term. The average person can then become functionally disordered in some degree and subservient to subconscious feelings of fear and hope, the two great destroyers of reason. The cumulative effects of the tension and frustrations of a hedonistic attitude give rise to the motivation for escape from the afflicted state of mind the average person finds himself in. This motivation then becomes the root of the desire to seek and enter into alternative states of existence or into altered states of mind.

An individual desires to attain an altered state of mind because such a state offers an alternative to remaining in the usual unsatisfactory state of mind. The desire to be free from the discontent of oppressing conditions of the mind and feelings is at the root of escapist behaviors like the need for constant entertainment, busy-work or play, captivating distractions of all sorts, social chattering, daydream fantasies, television addiction, alcoholism, drug addiction, and many more. Individuals develop phobias, or fears, of being alone, sitting still, being silent, and they get absorbed throughout each day in these obsessive behaviors and are motivated primarily by the stress of a restless mind. Even when filling the waking hours with multiple and continual escapisms, the phobic individual still feels unsatisfied, incomplete, or at least bored. There always seems to be yet something unfulfilled or incomplete. And these are feelings of stress and subconscious anxiety, so the individual keeps on seeking alternative states to counter the usual feelings generated by neurosis, psychosis, boredom, lethargy, sorrow, despair, grief, fear, hope, and all the rest of the unwanted experiences and states of mind which permeate life in some degree, from slight to overwhelming. These are the circumstances and conditions that create gloom, and everyone seeks to be free from this.

It is entirely futile to pursue the final overthrow of an unwanted aspect of existence in favor of its opposite. Evil cannot be overthrown by the domination of good; pain cannot be overthrown by the domination of pleasure. But the turmoil and the struggle persist, seemingly without any end or finality. If any end to the struggle is possible then it will not come as a result of incorporating a strategy concerning a warfare between the opposites with the intent that the good and pleasurable should finally dominate or destroy the evil and the painful. All the turmoil and warfare will end only when the apparent phenomenal conditions are understood as-they-really-are. Then the presumed dilemmas will also be known as-they-really-are and then transcendence can occur. All conditions will be seen as dependent upon other conditions, an infinite flux of event-conditions. But when any supposedly single condition is thought to be an independent entity unto itself, then it becomes desirable or undesirable and preference and prejudice then create the warfare.

What is generally not understood clearly is that no desire can be fulfilled because of the temporality of all phenomenal aspects of existence. What is objectively obtained will again be lost. Distracted and ignorant, the common man is aroused to seek fulfillment in the temporary, becoming distracted and obsessed, motivated to the commitment to false views concerning the world and existence in it. Not finding the presumed satisfaction, he maintains a constancy of bewilderment, fear, and delusion, locked into a cul-de-sac of turmoil, forever seeking strategies to escape therefrom. But no strategy will work so long as the problem is not clearly understood. If one has really understood the true condition as-it-really-is then one may cease to support the illusions and thereby cease to be affected by them. Nescient persons will continue to support and generate illusion and misunderstanding, increasing and sustaining the turmoils and torments. Only one who awakens can transcend the effects of the turmoil.

What is that something remaining unfulfilled or incomplete that motivates the search for ways to escape from the unsatisfactory conditions and situations? It is the only thing of real importance and if it is obtained the search for alternative states and other temporary gratifications would cease. The unceasing search itself is the constant evidence and reminder of dis-ease and unfulfilment, but most people have not discovered or realized what exactly is subconsciously felt to be missing in life. That which is at the root of escapist tactics is the anxiety which is an effect created by stultified individual evolutionary progress. When any individual, for any reason, is not motivated to strive toward his next stage of evolutionary progress, whatever stage that may be, he will feel the gloom generated by his own conscience, his personal indicator of something wrong, something out of order. Conscience is the silent voice which warns of disharmony in any moral context, and the prime moral agenda of all individuals is to progress to the next level or stage of their evolution. When this is not being done, the feeling of gloom becomes so uncomfortable that any distraction away from it becomes desirable. Then the individual seeks escape and relief by becoming absorbed in those activities which eventually only complicate the original root problem. Thus, the motivation at the root of the desire to enter into altered states is to escape from or suppress the feelings of gloom produced by not heeding conscience when it warns of avoidance of evolutionary responsibility.

CHAPTER TWO
THE ANALYSIS

Ignorance is a mental condition, a simple lack of meaningful knowledge, wherein an individual remains in a bewilderment due to an absence of understanding. Ignorance is non-knowledge that prevents a proper mental grasp of the reality of things, just as an absence of air would prevent breathing. Ignorance is a lack of comprehension that obscures the functions of perception and intelligence. The only way to properly conceive of ignorance is to relate it to an absence of knowledge, wisdom, or intelligence. The fullness of perceptive clarity is opposite to ignorance; it is lucidity, sanity, and clear intelligence.

Ignorance cannot be equated with the many varieties of false knowledge and wrong knowledge, for whatsoever form knowledge may exist in, it is still knowledge. False knowledge is the effect of mistaking a falsehood for a truth; wrong knowledge is the effect of a complex aberration of the faculty of discernment wherein a person gets confused by accepting partial evidence as the whole truth, or unverified assumption as fact. Wrong knowledge is an accumulated collection of information that has not been correctly discerned. False and wrong knowledge are conceptual presumptions and ideas that simply are not true in some degree, from partial untruth to complete untruth. Whether partial or complete, the deviation from truth is an outcome of irrational or defective discernment. Irrationality is the basis for the sustenance and continuity of all wrong knowledge and false views.

False views are incorrect conclusions determined through faulty reasoning processes. False views always result in the continuation of habitual delusive thinking, the flow of mistaken perceptions and judgements, chronic mental-sets, and all the associated consequences. The only way to eradicate false views is to understand their falsity and replace them with truth; this can be accomplished only by the development of unflawed reasoning. Faulty reasoning is the result of unsound and inaccurate observation and its consequent defective discernment. These are the mental conditions always antecedent to any and all subsequent incorrect conclusions made in thinking. If these obstructive mental conditions were absent, thinking would be purified and irrationality would disappear. In contrast, correct observation, the recognition of things as-they-really-are, and correct discernment, the clear perception of the qualities of things, is the state of lucidity.

All correct conclusions are the product of rational determinations founded upon verified facts and established evidence. Facts are verified and evidence is established through direct knowing experience rather than through rash inference, theory, or belief. Rash inference is reckless assumption, a habit of misperception that evolves from deficient, distorted, or incomplete observation. A theory is a speculative formulation of ideas based on observed phenomena or upon past theories and conjectures. If the observations are unsound or partial then discernment will be defective. Accepting something as a belief is the mistake of getting theoretical assumptions, inferences, and hypothetical conjectures confused with what is real, factual, and true. Thus, the whole process of thinking can get clouded and obscured, some degree of delusion always pollutes the function of reason, and then what is correct and true cannot be properly determined.

Passive acceptance without verification through sincere inquiry, and in the same way, rejection without inquiry and verification, is the activity of delusion. Delusion is the activity of mistaken thinking with lack of reason, believing or accepting that something is true when it actually is not. With reason and clear judgement the contradictions in errant thinking could be corrected. Contradiction is the established evidence of faulty conjecture stemming from unsound and inaccurate observation and discernment, and from impulsive acceptance or rejection.

Dogmatists and theoreticians readily proclaim their opinions regarding things accepted or rejected by them, having not sincerely or logically inquired into nor verified the actual status of that upon which they form their opinions. Their beliefs are based on wrong knowledge or on hopes and conjectures of imagination instead of direct knowing experience. Such beliefs are formulated from a faith which is itself built upon a foundation of conjecture based on hearing or reading about something; this is an acceptance of second-hand information. Such information is indirect knowledge and may be either true or false. Faith is imaginative conjecture, a consoling, hope-based conclusion determined aside from verified facts and without established evidence. A profession of faith is a confession of aberrant reason, an admission of faulty judgement. People who cling to faith do not usually bother to validate the procedure they have used to come to their conclusions.

True sanity is a sound mind capable of properly observing and accurately discerning. Observation entails the unobstructed and clear functions of the organs of sense perception;

discernment entails the synthesis of sense knowledge and the integration of sense data in all their relevant details in order to make valid and meaningful determinations of the evidences so gathered. Unsound minds rely upon incomplete or distorting mental processes, and these can proliferate into mental disorders and derangements in ever greater degree. Such disorders are commonly defined as insanity and delusion. Insanity is absence of sane judgement, a crippled capacity of the observing and discerning mind. The unreal then gets mistaken for the real, and the untrue is thought to be true. Doubt, confusion, frustration, grief, and superstition are the inevitable results of accepting fiction as fact. Not bothering to inquire or investigate is a passive act of self-victimization, a resignation unto ignorance and utter foolishness. Those who have allowed themselves to become slaves to imagination, superstition, or fanatical obsession with anything can expect only an increasing level of confusion, bewilderment, frustration, more conflict in living, and a coarse binding of intelligence.

Just because something is heard or something is written does not make it true or real. Falsehoods, lies, and some dogmas become acceptable to those who fear truth, or to those who find solace in falsehood, having done no critical reasoning for themselves. They have come to fear truth because of their obsession with vanity. But when truth is known ignorance must collapse; as vanity is a product of ignorance, it dissolves away also. Remaining in the bondage of ignorance and confusion is inevitable as long as vain fantasies and compulsive fascinations are held dear. The fear of death is coincident with the fear of confronting reality, both fears compounded by a third fear of losing a long-cherished dream based in a false faith or belief. Everyone has the option to believe whatsoever they please, but their mistakes of irrationality cannot alter the true or change the real. Expressions of foolishness follow along in the shadow of false views forever until truth is known and accepted as-it-is and all hallucinated fictions are discarded.

False views are reprehensible and pernicious; they are the foundation of errant motivation and wrong conduct and are the obstructions to lucidity. The eradication of ignorance and false views leads to the establishment of lucidity; this is the key to real contentment and happiness. In the absence of lucidity an individual actively consigns himself to self-victimization, a mechanical, habitual enslavement to the survival-level order of nature. This level of existence is a bondage ruled by a condition of mind that remains permeated by attachment, habits, compulsion, biases, and other mental activities of the semi-conscious unevolving person. On the other hand, lucidity is awakened, intelligent presence, a spontaneous and unfabricated awareness uncomplicated by the mechanistic conditioning of the mind. When lucidity is absent there is little clarity or presence in any aspect of individual consciousness. Absence of lucidity is the common state of being of the average human being.

This absence supports fixation in mechanistic automatism. The absence of lucidity is the basis for the development of fixations, which are obsessive attachments and habitual, semi-conscious compulsive preoccupations. A fixated individual is nearly continually and unknowingly vulnerable to the conditioning of environmental influences, social pressures, economic, political, religious, and cultural thought formats. When some degree of desire and attachment with such ideational formats is experienced, identification with them grows and crystallizes. Obsessive identification with outer conditions produces a seeming separation from inner realities. The focus between outer and inner becomes unbalanced and the result is always more unbalance, affliction, confusion, frustration, or some type of conflict. Then, when crystallized identification with these types of conditions occurs there is a further enhancement of subtle negative internal superficialities. Without developed capacity to evolve beyond compulsive fixation with coarse external and subtle internal superficial propensities, the individual must remain in the bondage and limitations of mechanistic automatism. Mechanistic automatism is impulsive, pre-patterned, conditioned reactivity in the individual mental apparatus which produces its associated effects in the external world through physical and emotional activities. Thus, conditions in the outer world are reflections of the conditions prevalent in the inner mental and emotional states. When such conditions become a fixed pattern they create a fixation, a mental-set.

The mental-set is the accumulated and fixed mental pattern of perspectives and opinions formed from repeated exposure to conditions of environment. These accumulated mental patterns form a stream of ideas based on either correct or on errant inferential supposition. Errant inferential supposition has its origin in the undeveloped capacity for correct discernment. Any inference is only superficial guesswork, a possibility of some degree. Without credible establishment of evidence through correct observation there can be only inferential supposition or imaginative ascription, which is concept-only. Then what is merely conceptual imputation can be easily mistaken for fact. Mistaking supposition for fact presents a nearly insurmountable obstacle to the development of any reality-based understanding. Any foundational errant supposition is the structural basis for endless subsequent errant perceptions, observations, discernments, and conceptualizations which result in a mental-set of nescient false views. Thereafter, all thinking and perspective become

24

tainted by the mental and emotional impressions of memory fabricated through lack of proper discernment, and will at some time eventuate in the circumstances of living within a perpetually recycling matrix of suppositional delusion and the consequent outcome of mechanistic automatism. Objects and events cannot then be known as-they-really-are and delusion will persist until all the perceptual and cognitive filters and obstructions based on errant supposition are dissipated. Errant supposition is a mental poison and keeps the mind non-lucid.

The non-lucid mind is an automaton of the metamorphic matrix. The mental equation of the unevolving individual is beset with chronic conceptual fixations, but he is not usually aware of this fact. In the inattentive and non-introspective person fixations and their consequent results develop mechanically, according to a definite ordered process. All of phenomenal nature is a living mechanistic organism in which causal factors result in definite associated effects, and these effects then become causes producing their subsequent future effects, ad infinitum. In the same way, the human mind, as a biologically functional nature-apparatus, operates in a definite conditioned mechanical pattern. Chronic nescience is similarly a natural product of a definite conditional mechanism which keeps the mind non-lucid. The metamorphic matrix is thus the mechanical level of coarse and subtle objective existence which produces itself out of itself, and which we perceive as visible, detectable nature, the worlds, and the universe.

Every structured complexity of objective being is only what it actually is, a mechanistic event-process of movement within the realms of phenomenal relativity. Everything has the same subjective base and so all things and events are a movement of flux and change within a multiplex field of scales of relativity. The mental functions of any individual are parts of scalar fields of change and like all the other parts are subject to change, restructuring, conditional morphation, and patterning. Subtle and gross phenomena in the processes of event-fluxation are the perceptual conditions for the operations of the human mind, the consciousness within which these matrix events arise, so consciousness and objective things and events are an interdependent causal process completely immersed within the same holistic identity.

The worlds and universe as well as individual sentient beings are mechanistic, without an inner objective self which is separate from the rest of objectivity. The absolute subjectivity is not a differentiated internal entity which inhabits phenomenal things or is located somewhere within a sentient individual. The absolute subjectivity is immanent and transcendent, both absolute and relative, both noumenon and phenomena. There is nothing other than It. To realize the coalescence of all apparent dualities is to be free of the conceptual implications and limitations of the phenomenal universes and the vehicles of sentiency. This is perfectly obvious to one who has developed ratiocinative certainty of understanding through experience. This kind of understanding is not a product of the mere intellect; nonetheless it must come through the intellect and conventional knowledge by way of ratiocinative analysis until the certainty of understanding crystallizes. Eventually, in this way, the intellect then can non-conceptually intuit the truth of existence as coalescent subject-object.

All perceivable objects and events are movements of vortex energies, either swirling or linear in their interdependent motions, and patterned fractal holons in microcosmic diminution of the macrocosmic holographic energy of consciousness itself. Each fractal holon is a microcosmic copy of the macrocosmic hologram. The universal hologram has no existence separate from the multitude of individual holons and no holon is separate from the universal or from other holons; thus homogeneity and heterogeneity are identical. All relative phenomena co-emerge and co-exist within an interdependent and integrally operating functional matrix of objects and events in spatiotemporality. Each holon is an imagery of the whole hologram and identical to it in its essence, yet each holon has the power to create change throughout the whole hologram. Thus, individuality is relative heterogeneity while at the same time being essential homogeneity. Morphic, or changing-and-adapting qualities of all apparently individual objects and events are simply formative structural patterns and conditional limitations continually arising and dissolving within the flux of the integrated matrix of the totality of existence. The totality of all the apparently individual things in existence is an interrelated unity of functional processes in conditioned mechanical patterns.

Mechanistic automated patterning eventuates in dichotomous perception. This is the mental patterning that inhibits or organizes all of a person's thinking; it is the unnoticed format and filter through which all perceptions and concept-makings are structured. The patterned structure of impressions in the subtle memory record always adds something of the mental-set to otherwise untainted perceptions and discernments, just as ignorance always leaves out something from lack of correct knowledge. The effect produced by mechanistic automated patterning in the mind is called dichotomous perception. Dichotomous perception occurs when the dysfunctional, non-lucid mind divides objects and events into presumed conceptual singularities which the perceiver, in his errant thinking, does not understand as actual integral relationships in a functional unicity of the phenomenal metamorphic matrix. Since there is really no such thing as a separately existing or exclusively self-produced phenomenon, the dichotomizing intellect is obviously mistaken in its dualistic presumptions. What is usually thought of as an object separate from other objects or events is a mistaken thought, an errant conceptual illusion, a delusory idea of pseudo-existence based on suppositionary mental formulas which add to and leave out basic verities. The primary basic truth or verity is the fact of functional unicity. Although seemingly individual things in the objective realms may be supposed to exist substantially as entities unto themselves, apart and different from other seemingly individual things and events, in fact, all things co-emerge and co-exist as morphic conditions in the incessant fluxing of the universal holographic matrix. All objectivity is a phenomenal fluxing of integrated and interrelated energies, so all objects and events are reciprocal, mutual, and complimentary. A change occurring anywhere within the universal holographic matrix produces a change everywhere therein.

Dichotomous perception is the chronic delusion which the individual must recognize and correct before understanding, or Gnosis can come about. Dichotomy, or dualistic perception, is a matter of illusive appearance-only, a product of irrationality, or undeveloped rationality, whereas lucidity is a matter of truth perception. At a deeper level, dichotomous perception can be equated with perceiver versus object of perception. This is also a dualism which is conceptual-only, having become a pervasively chronic habit of the non-lucid mind. This presumed dualism seems to exist only because the perceiver has not yet fully understood that all arises interdependently, even object and perceiver. But everyone gets absorbed in conceptual and perceptual dualisms, and then consciousness, because of attraction to some objects or repulsion from other objects, gets identified with particular objects and aspects of perception. The individual then begins to suppose he is a body-mind, a person that is a body and a mind – instead of that consciousness which is the pure perceiver of all objects, coarse or subtle, external or internal, within the phenomenal matrix. The individual forgets, or does not understand, that not only his body and mind arises from conditions of the matrix, but also the same is true of all "other" bodies and minds and all "other" consciousnesses. Even sense organs are, in each individual biological organism, functional objects of nature which mechanically transmit impulses and impressions to consciousness. Senses mechanically react to external stimuli and influences and then from this input of information the mind structures ideas and correlative pseudo-images, according to past psychological impressions and tendencies. Yet, in all formats of dualistic perception and consequent concept-making the perceiver and whatever is being perceived appear as a presumed duality because dichotomous discrimination leaves out the recognition and understanding of functional unicity.

The act of perceiving is a universal function occurring when there is consciousness and objects of perception. The function of perceiving requires both object and perceiver together; there is no real plurality. Without this understanding perceptions are always subliminally tainted through the suppositions of dichotomy which always superimposes something unreal from the mind onto whatever is being perceived. Perceiving is a self-function of the universal matrix, and both consciousness and objects of perception are the polar aspects of this self-function. There is no real separateness, no absolute individuality, and no real dichotomy, but this errant discriminative process maintains the mental factors producing irrationality and the resultant afflictions of confusion of various sorts and permits an increasing potential, in an already aberrated mental-set, for irrational supposition and increasing delusion. But there are answers to these problems when the problems are recognized.

If we investigate into our real condition, we eventually recognize that we have long been under the influence of the presupposition that everything comes to be as a result of causation, that there may be an external creator or force behind all that happens.

Another related presupposition is that each individual is an autonomous being, or a self which is inhabiting a particular mind and physical body as the "true person" which is implicated by perceived individually separate intention or will. These are two presuppositions which are hidden in the mental-sets of nearly everyone. Only those who undertake thorough contemplative introspection will experience this revealing. Then it will be surely known that cause-and-effect seriality, as usual perceived, is only an appearance, a seeming reality to those who do not understand the mental overlays which are unconsciously always added onto perceptions. Neither causes nor their supposed effects are things in themselves. Neither is the feeling of being separately existing to be rationally considered as an individual "self". Apperceptive Gnosis is the knowledge that consciousness is the basis of all thought and all conditional events in the flux of the matrix and is itself not caused from an external source. Consciousness is inherently free and there is no ultimate necessity for it to be under the supposed bondage of illusion.

Freedom from the apparent bondage of the limitations and conditions of all phenomenal existence arises as the result of a radical and comprehensive understanding. This understanding concerns the totality of the matrix of existence, life and events in inconceivable flux. There is no single "creator" or "being", as a separate individual being prior to other beings, directing the matrix of events or initiating any special event as a cause producing further effects. But the essential nature of all existence, and subtle potentiality itself, does not change or create motion outside of itself. All flux and all conditions are modifications and transformations of that inconceivable essence Itself in spontaneous fluxing. Within and through all existence there is no separate independent thing or occurrence-condition which is beyond or apart from this essential potentiality. There is no thing related to it as an "other", and it can be comprehended neither as "the one" nor as "the many", nor both "the one and the many". As such it is simply not conceivable. But it is the reality and there is nothing but it or other than it. The totality of manifestation, as events, appears and disappears, assembles and dissolves, as inevitable spontaneous fluxing, without perceivable reason – an inevitable morphing of conditions in their infinite interrelationships. But no condition or event is ever independent of the totality of fluxing. Even the flux itself is no independent thing conceivable as a thing or as an object. It is Pure Event.

External to, or separate from objects, events, and conscious beings there is no independent causal factor or creative entity which chooses to produce any thing or event. All conditions which arise are inevitable, but no single condition or sets of

33

conditions are a necessity or are a crucial aspect of the matrix of flux, but exist only relative to all else in existence. What presently exists as conditioned events is nothing other than the modifications of previous event-fluxation spontaneously arising without any willful direction of an interested creator or cause which is independent of any and all conditions and events themselves. Conditions and events do not imply or contain any separate entity or force which moves them into manifestation. If this truth can be recognized then attention can be freed from the drama of ego-identification. This freedom or liberation is not a structure which results from the accomplishment of practices or transformation of human experience; it is merely the absence of delusion. The incessant fabrication of bewilderment and conflict is a structure which can never be overcome or transcended through any willful motivation or manipulation. Simple recognition of the truth is all that is needed. This is the essential understanding.

Inattentive dichotomous perception is the individual base propensity. Individuality is only so within the context of the totality of phenomenal relativity, so there is no absolutely separated individuality. The word "individuality" defines itself remarkably well when analyzed through its syllables. "Individ" means undividable or indivisible; "duality" means "two". So the word "individuality" really means "indivisible duality". This perfectly describes the actual state of being of anything; there is an apparent, but not absolute, duality or separation between two individual things, yet these things are not completely separate since their very being depends on all else that exists. No thing can arise into existence out of itself; it comes from conditions other than itself, hence, all relativity is "indivisible dualities". Any duality is only an apparent, but not real, appearance. The true state of all is nonduality. Thus, any supposed identity is merely conceptual-only because every individual is defined and identified by specific characteristics in relation with the characteristics of other individuals. Individual objects and events can then be considered to exist as the identity they seem to be only because they are not any of the other supposedly individual things that exist.

The characteristic internal and external qualities, inclinations, preferences, and biases of persons are accumulated as they are each subjected to the experiences of pleasure and pain. When experience is judged on the basis of attraction and repulsion to pleasure and pain received and transmitted by sentient processes of the psychosomatic organism, life becomes permeated by the overlay of accumulated tendencies and predispositions. These tendencies form a structure of mental processes, a patterned and conditioned mental-set based upon developed preferences and prejudices, biases, fixations, and obsessions. All these conditioning factors evolve into the characteristics of individual personality. Thereafter, when the individual becomes attached and identified with these propensities and proclivities, the impression "me" emerges as a notion; "others" also emerge. By not understanding the process of attachment and identification and the consequent errant notions of duality and absolute separateness, one begins to habitually and mistakenly believe he is a body-mind persona, contending with separate "others". The "me" quickly becomes conceptualized as separate from all "others" who are similarly misidentifying themselves. This happens in early childhood before a person has sufficient opportunity to develop a modicum of reason.

Considering oneself as a definitely independent and separate entity is nescient supposition. A person develops this notion because he has come to identify himself as a body and a mind with a history and unique qualities. Along with the dualistic notions of "me" and the "other" as separate objects comes the forgetfulness of the integral interdependence and relative mutual correlations within the flux of the holographic structures and processes of the matrix of Being. The individual base propensity is just this constant mechanical tendency to misidentify subjective perceiving consciousness with a particular object. To this activity is also added the superimposition of memories of past events and imaginative projections into future time. In all these mental dichotomizations and overlays what is left out of the cognitive sequences is the realization that there is a functioning occurring with perceiver and perceived as the two necessary conditions of that functioning. Perceiving as functioning is the event that is beyond all dichotomies. True understanding of the function of universal perceptual consciousness is the recognition of the interdependent relativity of all subject-object events within the unified field of energies of the metamorphic matrix. The dualisms seem to be real until understanding dawns. Through the processes of attachment and identification, which can occur only in the presence of non-understanding and in the absence of reason, an individual becomes easily convinced that he is a separated body-mind object, an ego, a persona, and this is the individual base propensity from which arises all delusion.

From this base arises the delusion called volition. Although the ego-notion has a sort of conventional usefulness in mundane relations and communications in the everyday social domain, as pertains to lucidity and awakening to perfect reality, the notion is the primary hindrance. This hindrance is a progressively conditioned artificial fault of the mental functioning which results in the creation of an hallucinated conceptual counterfeit, the ego, the "me", the false identity, with its characteristics endowed to it by the errantly operating imagination. All phenomena, external or internal, are functional movements, abstractions of the appearance of heterogeneic multiplicity in the matrix of patterned formations. All natural mechanisms are limited to the functional processes of action and reaction, and therefore no object within the mechanical structures of phenomenal existence can possess autonomous free will, or volition. But, such a notion commonly emerges in the aberrated movements of a mentality in which good reason is absent.

Pseudo-volition is a basic factor in the support structure of incessant fixations and delusions. All nescient delusion and its activities can create the discomforts and discontents of physical, emotional, and mental afflictions. Such afflictions perpetuate the cyclic recurrence of conflict brought on by reactive and compulsive mental movements. Even physical afflictions can be caused by a mental attitude strong enough to produce tension, stress, and disharmony in the nervous system of the human organism. Emotional afflictions can be caused by wrong thinking regarding any circumstance of the mundane world, its social interactions, and the resulting frustrations resulting from unfulfilled egoistic motivations. Mental afflictions arise from long-repeated formation and the deepening of psychological impressions, the intensification of mechanistic patterning through dichotomous thinking and its resultant delusions, and then the crystallization of the individual base propensity which then supports even more pseudo-volitional notions and motivations in the realms of activity. The active expressions of this pattern are all the afflictions of life which bind a person to the results of unconscious compulsion.

Absorption in compulsive delusion generates conflict. When patterned habitual mental sets become so deeply ingrained that the majority of thinking and conduct fall below the level of attentive awareness and into subconscious automatism, the individual becomes regularly absorbed in the compulsive and reactive levels of physical, emotional, and mental experience. Absorption means being engrossed, captivated, and perpetually locked into inattentive modes of passivity and distraction. Absorption is the deluded state of passivity of attention in which one is almost continually lost in dichotomous identity fixation and the activities of mechanistic automatism. Human beings, when thinking of themselves as their imaginary conceptual counterfeit, the ego, then believe their thoughts and subsequent actions are acts of a decided volition, or free will. But this cannot be true because individuals only react through the mechanics of stimulus within the limitations of conditional phenomena and the psychosomatic organism, and all completely within the chain of metamorphic cause and effect sequentiality.

Volition, or free will, that an individual may suppose he possesses as uncaused, unlimited, unbound, unconditioned, and free power of choice, cannot be and does not exist as such. The notion of volition unbound is an errant judgement and not true because every object and event within the various aspects of environments are factors of relative mechanical causality and result in the development of tendencies, propensities, and traits of personality and character. Any decision or supposed willful choice is inevitably linked to the multitude of conditions within the chain of causality. Choice-making which is totally and completely separate from conditions of the causal nexus cannot exist. The notion of free will rests upon the antecedent errant notion of ego, the base propensity. The deluded notion of having free will is another fundamental hindrance to the recognition of the true and the real. All volitional acts are always linked with accumulated mental propensities such as preference or prejudice, for-and-against attitudes of attraction and repulsion. However, a spontaneous act of free volition might be possible by beings who are not self-identified as egos, but this is an extreme rarity as there can be spontaneity only in the absence of compulsive absorption.

The chain of events generated by absorption leads always to conflict in some degree. All misery and turmoil in the life of any individual or in collective social groups is generated and spawned into existence inseparably entangled within the chain of conditioned events, from ignorance through resultant affliction until conflict. Just as the associated train of thought continues mechanically in the non-lucid mind, so also does absorption continue automatically in the same way, producing the continuity of conditioned afflictions and conflict.

Conflict is a natural link in evolutional metamorphic flux. The generation of conflict is innate in the integral relations and metamorphic processes throughout the fluxations of all the coarse and subtle phenomena of external and internal realms of existence. Metamorphic causality is an integrated matrix of cause-and-effect sequentiality whereby all objects and events are generated from the subtle inner realms outwardly, to be eventually manifested into the coarser external realms. The subtle inner realm of thought and image-making mental activities is the genetrix of all the phenomenal relativity which then becomes the basis for the generation of further subtle mental activity. Thus, a reciprocal mechanical process is actuated which continues sequentially until the process is interrupted.

All discernible events are temporal and in consciousness are extant only as a perceptive moment within the flux of conditional factors which also have no substantial fixed or permanent existence or being. Seen with correct discernment, objects are more like temporal integrated events rather than like things apart from other things. When disharmony on subtle levels eventuates in coarse events of affliction or conflict, an event matrix of functionality is established whereby resultant external phenomena become perpetuating agents, or localized patterns of flux, fluctuation, for the further deepening, extension, and sustenance of nescient misunderstanding and ever more fixated absorption. The integral flow of this event matrix is entirely mechanical and is the basis for the eventual development of the individual's desire to escape from or to avoid the turmoil and adversity of its conditions. This is the desire to be free from the trap of perpetual absorption in the nexus of afflictive predicaments and a bewildered life, in whatever degree, and the core of the insatiable longing to discover that which will give relief from the turmoil and conflict experienced in life. It may be asked if anything good can come of this type of negative situation. The positive answers follow.

CHAPTER THREE
BREAKTHROUGH

The conflict nexus eventually begets the rational mind and this marks a critical point of breakthrough toward the emergence of individuated holistic intelligence. Some individuals are thoughtful enough to be curious about their existence and its purpose, or to inquire into whether or not there may even be a purpose. Neither searching for nor finding answers to basic questions regarding purposeful existence, and thus not satisfying their primal curiosity and longing, individuals fall into distress, bewilderment, and all the unsatisfactory conditions of anxiety which ignorance sustains. Any individual who is curious about the real implications of purposeful existence must eventually comprehend that all confusions and doubts are rooted in that ignorance. Symptomatic stresses such as frustration and anxiety are generally submerged in the lower subconscious levels of mind and memory where they cannot be confronted or examined clearly. So, in a bewildered attempt to counter the effects of frustration and anxiety, individuals and groups become attracted and attached in identity with various formats of false or partial values, false religions, superstitious beliefs, misconceptions of all sorts, and the inevitable delusive compulsion will further beset them. The pursuit of the false, the insignificant, and the valueless produces thereafter a morose and unhappy life. Those with undeveloped capacity for reason cannot understand the difference, in some cases, between the true and the false, or between the significant and the insignificant. Only through the development of a rational mind can recognition of verities and clear understanding progress. The continuity of conceptual delusion negates any possibility for reason or rationality to be developed; it is the absence of rational thinking which nourishes and sustains the motivation to believe in the dogmatic suppositions of religious theories or pseudo-science without relying on proven facts and established evidence.

Individuals who participate in such delusions are seeking to escape from the turmoils of frustration and from the tensions of anxiety and all the afflictions associated with those. People become seekers of a futuristic glorious existence in a faraway celestial realm because they desire to escape their present world of anxiety, fear, gloom, and dissatisfaction inherent in the always temporary and dissolving experiences of seeking an always receding happiness.

This is the common mental-set of the average person who attempts to override feelings of discomfort and insecurity with replacements of physical, emotional, and psychological gratifications. All motives for seeking such forms of gratification are obvious manifestations of pseudo-volition directed toward egoic security based on feelings of fear; the seeker wants to counter the fears by adopting hope – the placebo for fear – all of which is dysfunctional and unevolved concept-making.

When the individual realizes that his conflict status is nearly perpetual, broken only by short gaps of pleasure or pleasure-seeking and associated temporal fulfillments, then he reaches a critical point in the real progress of his personal evolution. At this point the individual begins to consciously strive with determination to try to understand the real causes and processes which contribute to his afflicted condition. For him this is a new and purposeful motivation of significance which gives birth to a restructuring of thought processes along lines of rational sequence. Sequential, rational thought is active, linear concept-making, and when grounded in established facts and evidence, can correctly observe patterns of cause and effect. These patterns then become more evident and familiar, obvious in the sense observations and reasoning of the individual. Sequential, linear thought eventually matures into the capacity for multi-referencing matrix thinking that can recognize the integral, interrelated functioning of the matrix of existence. Thus, the conditions of conflict in the nexus of the existential matrix induce the individual to seek relief and escape from unsatisfactory modes of existence, and this eventually culminates in an intolerable crisis which begets the rational mind. This crisis is the realization that unsatisfactory and painful existence cannot be ended until the foundational structures and their operative sequential effects that are creating the conditions of conflict are recognized and then interrupted or dissolved entirely away. The origins and structures of any aspect of the conditional nexus can be determined only through rational thinking. The capacity for rational thinking increases in degrees diametrically equal to the capacity for maintaining concentrated attentiveness to specific topics, objects, and events, and how they are related and interrelated within conditioned flux in the totality of the phenomenal matrix. In this manner, skill in purposeful attentive focus is developed, the rational mind takes its birth, and evolutionary progress resumes.

Having consigned oneself to the path of progress, it is then concomitant that one meets with great teachers and helpers along the way. These people may be anyone, even the most ignorant and ignoble, yet to one who perceives at a higher level of Gnosis, all are teachers since they represent conditions to be fully understood. Also in one's travels along the way there come to light great and profound texts left from antiquity to those who may in future times profit from the knowledge that great adepts and masters have recorded in them. Most importantly, all the knowledge and instruction one may gain through accumulated learning in esoteric subjects and their pragmatic application in daily living, is the fact that progress is more rapidly made by the acts of subtraction rather than addition. There are many and various obstructions and pitfalls on the way, some so obnoxious as to nearly curtail any further progress – or even set the traveler into a reversal – an entanglement within degenerative activities. The modus operandi of an adept traveler on the way, therefore, is to subtract these obstructions by identifying and realizing their detrimental effects. The most harmful of obstructions are false views. False views are simply eliminated by recognizing their falsity. Nothing has to be added to one's knowledge; no addition need be pursued. All the teachers, helpers, and texts of real value always teach the art of subtraction, transcending delusions. To do this efficiently, one must by necessity learn the art of dialectic reasoning to the level of perfect ratiocination.

Willful attentive skill develops exacting ratiocination. Willful attentive skill is the capacity to be developed for the elimination of ignorance and nescience from the non-lucid mind. When trying to

47

understand what mind and consciousness really are, an individual starts looking inward at his own subtle internal functions; he finds that his fundamental perceptual awareness is virtually always in motion, involved in acts of momentary attention and concept-making. This is called mind. When these instants of attention are mechanical and automated to the level of reactivity, they are not a willful placement of attention, but the reactive activities of ingrained, mechanistic automatism. This is lax, passive attention to any object or event; it is habitual distraction and semi-conscious reactiveness. On the other hand, active attention is willful attentiveness toward a specifically selected object, event, or topic, a purposefully placed, deliberate focusing of attention. Active attention is the determined directing of concentration, whereas passive attention is the semi-conscious reactive mode of awareness, perceptivity gone astray and lost in the automated distractions of daydreaming and semi-sleep.

Both of these aspects of attention, passive and active modes, are necessarily confined to some object, but only active attention is the mode of awareness defined by deliberate placement. In the developmental stages of the evolving individual, the only real volition, or willful choice, is the choosing of a suitable idea or object for inspection and perhaps for analysis; doing so, it is suspected, may somehow benefit the contemplator by producing knowledge.

The most important benefit, however, will be the development of an exacting ratiocinative ability. Until this point of recognition in the personal evolution of the individual there has previously been no significant willful placement of attention regarding the operations and functions of the perceptual and thinking processes. The motivation to develop the ability for willful attentive skill, or mindful reflection and contemplation is the initial essential factor required for the higher development of exacting ratiocination. Ratiocination is the highest level of scrutiny in rational conceptualization and the only possibility for superseding the limitations of nescience and errant suppositions. Only the exacting ratiocinative mind can be used to understand the mechanics of disharmony and the mechanics of harmony. Therefore, the development of the exacting ratiocinative capacity of the mind is crucial, for without this development there can never be any certainty of understanding or recognition of truth.

Only recognition can disrupt absorption in delusive compulsion. Whether or not the individual understands and recognizes the truth does not change reality; whether or not the individual understands and recognizes the truth does not stop the mechanism of the causal nexus. But understanding and recognition can disrupt absorption in delusive compulsion which is a component of the dysfunctional psychological apparatus. The continuity of presumptuous thought based on falsehood or conjecture must be broken. A gap or break in the continuity of the incessant perpetuity of delusion and distraction has to be intentionally created. This gap is then slowly nurtured and matured until it is no longer a short gap in the long uninterrupted flow of distraction and semi-consciousness; with practice this can become a total absence of distraction. The absence of nescience, along with the absence of distraction in semi-conscious passive attention is the vital prerequisite for achieving unbound free consciousness in lucidity. When there remain moments of nescient thought construction and traces of semi-conscious distractedness then there is yet a lack of perfect attentive skill. With the maturation of willful attentive skill comes the disruption of absorption.

Long-repeated disruption eventuates in attentive stabilization. Disruption of the absorption in nescient thought processes is critical and is begun by creating gaps in inattentiveness. Inattentiveness is disrupted by fostering short moments of attentiveness. The basis of nescient dualistic concept-making and distracted inattentiveness is the base propensity, the ego-notion. The objectifying of one's subjectivity is the dichotomy of errant perception to be transcended, and one who has stabilized his attention perfectly does not fluctuate back into conceptual aberration. This means one must learn to detect and recognize the very beginnings of distraction and gain a decisive understanding of its mechanics. When automated, reactive concept-making, the usual daydreaming, is stopped by attentiveness to present mental situations themselves, always based on the ego-notion, then the ego-notion will simultaneously subside and automated thought activity will stop. This is the nondual, nondichotomous realization of one's true identity as pure consciousness but possible only in the total absence of the counterfeit identity, the base propensity, ego.

As long as one continues to suppose he is an ego and others are egos – considered as separate body-mind entities, then everything else in the objective realms will be automatically presumed to exist as separate, isolated entities also. The only way to promote the absence of repetitive fluctuation between lucidity and semi-conscious daydream activity is to attentively continue to create gaps in the continuity of distraction. With practice these gaps can be expanded so that eventually they last longer than the continuity of distraction. Lucidity becomes the continuity when the influences of nescience and semi-conscious daydream activity have been eradicated and when the five aspects of consciousness activity are no longer in differentiation.

To achieve stabilization in lucidity it is necessary to understand the different aspects of consciousness activity. These five are:

Lucidity
Waking thought
Waking dream
Dream sleep
Deep sleep

The life of the individual is focused in one or the other of these aspects throughout every day and night. With the achievement of the continuity of lucidity the first four differentiated aspects of consciousness activity are integrated into holistic lucidity. Holistic lucidity is the very ground of being and existence, timeless and spaceless, beyond all causality. With lucidity one experiences the silent depth of presence.

In waking thought consciousness one is usually focused on coarse external phenomena with willfully directed thought. In waking dream one is focused in the mechanical mental mechanism of daydream activity with the senses semi-functional. In both the waking thought aspect and the waking dream aspect of consciousness activity there is only a semblance of actively directed attention. In dream sleep one is focused in the mental mechanism of dream while the body is immobile and the senses nearly non-functional. In both the waking dream and dream sleep aspects the focus is in the subtle internal realm of mental imagery. In deep sleep there is the silence of dreamlessness with no imagery and no thoughts; here the mind is without particular focus and no linear thought functioning. These four aspects of consciousness activity are differentiations from the fundamental primal lucidity. Lucidity itself actually is not an aspect of anything other than itself, nor does it emanate from any previous cause or condition. To see it as a fifth aspect of consciousness activity is not correct although it can so be conventionally described. Lucidity, or pure consciousness, is self-existent and eternal, the hidden intrinsic knowing essence of all and everything and everyone. Lucid pure consciousness is the truth of all existence; it is the only one subjective permanence. The other four aspects of it are its differentiations and permutations, but all essentially concomitant with one another.

Waking thought consciousness is the field of experience and creativity in the coarse phenomenal matrix, but with the common individual the waking state is not very wakeful at all; it is obfuscated and obstructed by the accumulations of impressions made by previous faulty perspectives and errant discriminations. These turn into tendencies and predispositions which are at the root of continuing nescience. People are almost constantly in a mixed state of awareness while awake, between dream sleep and waking thought; this is waking dream. Waking dream is the pervading daydream, a condition of sleep mixed in with the aspect of waking thought. Most persons are habitually absorbed in daydream throughout the majority of each day, so the waking thought aspect is actually ruled and obscured by an affliction of the mind, having become habitually mechanical, automated and warped by discriminative dysfunction. The afflicted individual does not recognize this as being his nearly continual condition of consciousness activity. Although most persons are convinced they are awake and aware, they do not recognize their superficial and mechanical condition of automatism. Theirs is a condition of confined consciousness, a mode of mental activity in which perceptive boundaries and the limitations of nescience become obstructions. In both daydream and dream sleep the mechanical tendency of the mind is to complete whatever has been left unconsummated and unfulfilled in the desire-nature of the individual.

Ego-based desire is at the root of frustration and frustration is a basis of stress and tension, so the mechanisms of the mind automatically formulate imaginative scenarios in dream sleep and in waking dream, creating a fantasy of imaginative fulfillment in order to lessen tension and relieve the effects of frustration so the nervous system of the physical organism can have a period of rest and temporary recuperation during and after each day of waking experience. In the waking state tension can be somewhat overridden or ignored, or perhaps temporarily suppressed when a person gets entangled in distraction or entertainment or in an obscuring daydream. Desires that have ego as their base engender these feelings of incompletion and unfulfilment, but upon the entering into dream sleep these tensions cannot be willfully suppressed and a dream display will unfurl itself in order to imaginatively complete the unfulfilled desire. Dream fantasies are unintentional, automatic, and mechanical, and they occur without willful act of attention; the dream sleep state is completely automated. Daydreaming and other distracted modes of attention are transcended when lucidity is present because lucidity is without ego; ego and dream are complimentary. Dreaming is ego-based but lucidity demands egolessness. In the state of lucid presence all dreaming must stop because the base for dreaming is absent.

When the fantasies of dream are known to be what they really are, there is a possibility for dreaming to be suspended and eventually terminated. Dreaming individuals live in lower desires, fears, anxieties, and delusion. When dreaming is regularly noticed in the waking aspect of consciousness activity it is the beginning of the path leading to dream purgation and the overcoming of delusion, but without awareness of these facts nothing can be done. With the development of attentive skill it will be noticed that nearly the whole day of so-called "waking" is spent absorbed in the flow of intermittent mechanistic automatism, the activity of propensities and tendencies that always are erupting in daydream displays. Becoming more and more continuously aware in a vigilant presence negates all dreaming and allows all the layers of subconscious patterns to dissipate through the portal of lucid waking presence. Becoming aware of daydream projections is the prerequisite to becoming aware also of dream sleep projective displays. This procedural sequence, developed only in the mature contemplative, is necessary in order to interject willful intent into the processes of waking dream, then into the dream sleep state. With practice and the development of contemplative skill, willful intent can become useful in the dream sleep aspect as a tool to eradicate unwanted impressions and patterns in the subconscious. One can, upon waking from a dream display in dream sleep, remembering it clearly, fall quickly back asleep with the intention to continue the scenario of the dream or "replay" it once again, making alterations and adjustments within it. In this way, parts of a dream which reveal unwanted, unsatisfactory, or unwholesome attitudes and tendencies can be replaced with action sequences based on virtuous intent. This is a powerfully effective contemplative device for progressively purifying the subconscious of obstructive impressions.

With skillfulness and stability in lucid presence all unintentional automated dreaming will eventually altogether cease. In the waking thought and waking dream aspects the ego-notion is dominant. In the dream sleep aspect the ego-notion is somewhat weaker; in deep dreamless sleep it is absent. Deep dreamless sleep is nearly total unawareness and unconscious dormancy in the non-contemplative common person. In waking thought, waking dream, and dream sleep, awareness always has an object of focus, but during deep sleep there is no object of focus, naught objective to be conscious of. Deep sleep is an absence of mental function because all thought and image projection are then suspended. If one can become truly aware in waking aspect with vigilant presence, then in the dream states this presence becomes dominant and the mechanistic dream activities cease; then the deep sleep aspect can also be consciously experienced with presence.

Thus, the differentiated aspects of consciousness activity can be integrated into holistic, lucid pure presence where there are no longer any differentiations or dichotomies whatsoever. Centered in this lucidity one has returned to his deepest primordial nature. Deeply within the truth of all being and existence, everything then becomes obvious in a holographic, totalistic perspective. This lucid pure consciousness is that from which all began, from which all is phenomenally manifest and apparently differentiated, in which all is contained, and to which all must obviously belong and be identical with. Lucid pure consciousness is the precursor of all apparent differentiation, coarse or subtle but is itself beyond all spatiotemporality, as well as being identical with it. It is the only constant reality. It is the only thing that does not change in its essence, yet it is the essence also of all flux and change in the totality of the existential matrix. It is absolute simplicity and at the same time absolute complexity, homogeneity as well as heterogeneity. To enter into the totalistic presence of the eternal and infinite, the evolving individual must learn to integrate lucidity with the other aspects of consciousness activity. The absence of nescience-based fluctuations within the differentiated aspects of consciousness activity is attentive stabilization.

Stabilization disengages the continuity of dichotomous perceptions. The individual who has become skillful in clear attentiveness and firm in purpose is no longer distracted and subservient to the conditions of nescience. The whole flow of dichotomous perception is disengaged from when an individual stabilizes attention and is not distracted or in the throes of daydream. In the absence of distraction the mind is not aberrated or susceptible to distortion, but can operate in present wakefulness. When disturbing afflictive attitudes are not present, then stabilized lucidity can be present. Attentive stabilization means not being engrossed in fixations of attention, but being constant and stable in non-fixated free attention. This stabilization thoroughly dismantles all structured impressions of delusion and the individual can then perfectly abandon attachment to habitual mechanical tendencies. In such clear perceptive attitude there is no preference or prejudice, no accepting or rejecting of external or internal events. When dualistic biases are absent all phenomena are recognized truly as interrelated components of the flux of the co-emergent matrix of objectivity. Stabilization in astute wakefulness is unconcocted, unconditional, totally open and receptive, and free of mechanical automatism.

When automated mechanisms of mentality fade, consciousness is freed. Continuous fixated activity belongs to those who are as yet unawakened and entangled in the incessant repetitive rounds of automatism. When consciousness in its differentiated aspects is associated with constrictive afflictions such as the ego-notion, delusion, and pseudo-volition it is bound up with obstructive limitations. This is the unevolved state of nescience. Since the pseudo-volitional stance of the unevolving individual mind is a semi-conscious state resulting from the lack of capacity for correct discernment, there must be a total submission, relinquishment, and abandonment of the inattentiveness which allows the structure-building of automatism. Then consciousness can be freed from all binding influences.

Consciousness is already the principle of all recognition and understanding, and inherent within consciousness is the potential to know that all objective conditions, subtle or gross, are modifications in fluxation. There is no single part or aspect of the flux which can be isolated as self-existent. All is a grand modification, an enormous infinite conglomeration of motion that appears to have some implication or purposeful final goal, indicated by the conventional "clash of the opposites" such as good and evil, happiness and sadness, war and peace. But there is no real dualism of opposition between the aspects of objective phenomenal fluxing in things or in beings. Nescient cogitation may mistakenly structure presumptions about absolute subjectivity, but as these presumptions are based in dichotomous perception they cannot reach to the understanding of Gnosis. Perceiving according to the occlusions of the senses and of the body-mind, or the errant conceptions of conditional factors of experience, one cannot recognize or realize clearly, or function in Gnosis. Instead of realization there is only imagination without certainty. This errant imagination produces the pseudo-reality that is thought to be actual and authentic. Therefore, those who remain without developed ratiocinative certainty become occluded with a false understanding of the apparently external world and an aberrated image of their own situation. This happens mechanically because of lack of reason and lack of proper analytical contemplation, so the understanding of reality as immanence and transcendence coalesced is impossible. It remains impossible to understand because it is approached in the same manner as the rest of experience is conceptualized – through the base-propensity of the ego-notion, according to desire and frustration, hope and fear, preference and prejudice, and all the other conceptual dualities of the body-mind. The body-mind cannot enclose understanding of the totality of the flux of the matrix, since it is an aspect of the flux itself, and is itself enclosed. It has been said that "the limited cannot understand the unlimited". But we say, "the limited is potentially unlimited".

There may be many different ways to "achieve" what is called enlightenment, hence so many different approaches or "paths". But near the end of the so-called "path" one inevitably comes to the realization that all "paths" are simply aspects of the one real great path. As there are many differentiated elements of the "path" so then there have evolved many coinciding formulas for reaching the understanding which is needed to proceed to the next "stage" along the "path". Primarily, in the upper extremities of the approaches to the "goal" one discovers there are basically two ways to find the "end" of the "path". The first way is to introspect

61

deeply into the functions and content of the mind. Finding there the many dysfunctions and obstructions to clear thinking and clear recognition one decides to develop ratiocinative abilities in order to determine the correct next "stage" of the "path". This probably also includes the replacement of unskillful mental qualities with skillful qualities, which takes much introspective effort. The second way involves a format of analytical thought and meditation whereby one eventually realizes a more obvious "way" or "path", which is to learn how to detach from the error of motivation for transformation of the sentient vehicles, including senses, body and mind, through "paths" or practices, and instead, at a higher level, re-seat oneself in the original primal Gnosis itself, transcending all motivation to seek by means of a "path" that supposedly goes from dualistic "here" to "there", and just relying upon the understanding and realizing of one's essential Gnosis, beyond all pseudo-identity which generates such motivations, and just remaining in the spontaneous apperceptive "seeing" of all there is as-it-really-is.

Free consciousness is individuated holistic intelligence with lucidity. Consciousness in the individual is just ordinary wakeful awareness in differentiated aspects. In its unrestricted, unconfined, and non-constricted state it is natural lucidity. This lucidity is the original, primordial, conditionless condition of free and pure consciousness. The individual, once having recognized his natural holistic presence, is then concerned with integrated wholes, or the total unfragmented system of objectifications within the manifesting matrix, rather than with deluded absorption in and attachment with the supposedly separate parts of it. All phenomena are then recognized just as-they-really-are, as interrelated components of the unified field of fluxing conditions in cause-and-effect sequentiality. This recognition is the precursor to undifferentiated nondual holistic lucidity in which all the implications of the afflictions of conceptual dualism have ceased to be, and the phenomenal matrix is clearly observed, cognized, and perfectly understood.

This primordial awareness is the unchanging principle of all changes; it can know all and it can know itself. This unconditional awareness is not just a blank mirror able to reflect images, but is the source of all knowledge, will, and action. It is sovereign unto itself and the supreme spiritual power, all-inclusive, both immanent and transcendent simultaneously. Everything starts as a potency within this source; all beings have this source as their own essential nature. This is the one essence from which all phenomena are derived and with which all phenomena are secretly identified. Since all phenomena whatsoever have this same essential nature then all phenomena are nondual, meaning that absolute diversity is only an illusory appearance; in whichever way something may seem to appear, its real essential nature cannot differ from this one universal source, and this quality of sameness is the fact of nonduality. All phenomena are beyond categorization by conceptual elaboration because the limited human mind cannot conceive all the infinite causal and relative correlations and all the endless details and possibilities inherent in the totality of conditional relations. The source is beyond conceptual elaboration since it is both immanent in and transcendent beyond each particular objective phenomenon or the totality of phenomenal existents. Elaboration and categorization by means of concepts and ideas cannot truthfully or completely represent the infinitude of conditional relativity, let alone the primordial source essence, the principle, which has no definable boundaries or limits of itself.

A contemplative practitioner does not have to create or change anything; he just recognizes his own consciousness in its unaltered true state. Alterations and corrections are functions of the dichotomizing mind absorbed in the delusions of dualisms. When examining the true primal state of consciousness holistic unity is recognized; everything has the same source, permeating all places without boundaries.

This essence always retains its own self-nature without change, yet always adapts and establishes beings; it is omnipresent, eternally pure, and pervades all times, but cannot be explained with words. It is not something that can be cultivated.

CHAPTER FOUR
THE SOLUTION

Our theme is Gnosis, and this is direct primordial enlightenment, so now we speak directly to you, the reader, as Gnosis is an individual, personal experience. You must make a passage from ignorance through learning to wisdom. There must be an opening away from the profane into the transcendental which is also the immanent, your immanency. You are this immanency, free already from profane distortion; you are the most ordinary, functional innate consciousness, only needing to self-recognize yourself. The divine life is at the very root of the profane, made profane only by distortions in the thinking and perception as described before. The innate state of consciousness which you are is not only the source of your mind but also the source and nature of all the moving phenomena which come and go throughout all of cyclic existence. This great blissful consciousness is that generating all beings and things and environments – all already pure in essence. As long as you do not understand your own

67

nature, your own real reality, you will remain a common sentient being; but when understanding, all becomes clear. You will know what you really are. The difference between conflict and freedom depends on whether or not you are obscured about your real reality. It will do no good to keep thinking about it and trying to figure it out. You must know that when conceptualizing stops, non-conceptual awareness is present. You are exactly that in your primal state.

You can simply observe thoughts; this is called mind. If you vigilantly watch for thoughts to arise, remaining receptive to their potential arisings, they don't then arise. What is watching vigilantly for them to arise is the source from which they come, your pure essence. The distinction between mind and pure consciousness has to be made. When thoughts do arise, without following along entangled in them, they can simply be observed, and upon directly looking at them, or for them, they dissolve by themselves back into their source. You are just a knowing mirror, wisdom beyond mind. The relationship between your inherent wisdom-consciousness and the thought-filled dichotomizing mind is like the reflective capacity of a mirror and the reflections that continually arise upon it. You have to learn to work with this movement and get deeply experienced with it. In pure presence there is no difference between the calm state of mind and the movements of thoughts. If thoughts come up, be present in awareness of that; if no thoughts happen to appear, whatever happens, be presently aware of that. Whatever happens, there is a spontaneous presence beyond either movement or non-movement.

After you prepare yourself to recognize yourself as fundamental primordial awareness in contradistinction with the automaton mind, holistic unity then can become obvious. Stability comes about through recognizing again and again your primordial base and learning to relax into that presence. A higher kind of knowledge is therein, transcending the distortions of mind. Contemplation is the relaxation of that mind completely until a relaxed presence continues steadily. Everything is known as a distinct manifestation of the energies of your basic state and therefore all is known as fundamentally pure. There is no need to try to purify anything. Then you can relax, and this relaxation requires no intention. You are already where you might have been previously motivated to get to, so this state is obviously already pure. You only need to learn to remain relaxed in presence no matter what the events and circumstances appear to be as outcomes of the infinite arisings of energy. You learn to integrate your conduct with this state of wisdom and presence. Everything that happens becomes an opportune occasion to practice removing obscurations by letting them self-dissolve away. Contemplation like this does not require a modification of anything, and presence is integrated with all events which continually come and go; there is an absence of tension or any effort of trying to relax. Thought movement subsides and mental agitation wanes. All are seen and known as aspects of totalistic existence; this is equanimity, vigilant relaxed presence with wisdom, undistracted.

No matter what happens, you don't have to let it distract you. No matter what occurs either externally or internally, coarsely or subtly, it has no power over you. You need not continue to be caught within the causal nexus. Just one instant's recognition of primordial source consciousness eradicates negative habitual propensities and mental hindrances accumulated over all past time. Primordial essence cannot be tainted by multitudinous delusions. This stainless consciousness is the Gnosis. Gnosis here and now is the summum bonum of all meditative and contemplative exercise, the end of all ratiocinative growth, and erupts in spontaneous pure and right conduct. When the mind is free of hope and fear, you are sovereign and free. Whatever comes to be, just let it be so, without any interference, without criticism, evaluation, preference, or prejudice. Presume nothing at all. This is pure perspective beyond all striving based upon egoistic motivations. The base propensity, ego, is no longer your base; your base is primal awareness. As phenomena arise, just let them be, leave them as they are and don't get attached; defilements of mind are naturally free to dissolve because of absence of attachment to them.

This contemplation is the innate experience of being free and with intense and prolonged practice all motivational illnesses will vanish. The constant emergence of vivid events and appearances is a continuous wonder when you can just be this way. Stay poised, free and easeful, in a state of perception where there is no residue of mind and proclivities and become stable in unfixated relaxed presence. If mental residue arises, just let it go its own way, staying aware in detached equanimity. Stay awake in acute presence and lucidity, not in some kind of absorbed trance, but in brilliant presence of right here and right now. You don't have to try to alter your thoughts in any way; just leave them alone to do whatever they do without clinging to them or rejecting them. After all, they are perfect results of the holistic matrix, and as such are naturally pure in their own way. Your wisdom will extract the pervasive energies of aberrant thought and change it into divine energy.

When this source state of lucid awareness is recognized, it is that very awareness which is recognizing itself. But this experience is very different from all other perceptual experience because here the perceiver is not perceiving an object. The perceiver perceives itself and recognizes objectless perception. One recognizes oneself as already self-perfected and as such, all barriers are spontaneously overcome. Tensions are relaxed until they dissolve away, and proper conduct in pure presence according to wisdom is then also spontaneous. Seeing the perfection of cause and effect sequentiality everything is then known to be already perfectly accomplished. Obligation and personal efforts arise from egoistic agitation and tension created by the deluded automaton mind; these things are like an illness. All the activities of daily life can be integrated within the state of formless contemplation, this state of pure awareness. It may be necessary to calm the mind a bit first if it is absorbed in habit energies, and then just stably abide in the recognition of holistic lucidity. The contemplative practice is to remain relaxed and cognizant of how mental conditions and factors come and go, along with their feelings, emotions, and all distractive external objects and events, while simultaneously recognizing them all within the context of the flux of the totality of the matrix. This is holistic wisdom. The more this is done, the more realization crystallizes that all thoughts and superimpositions arise from source consciousness and reenter into it. Thoughts themselves are of the essence of pure primordial awareness and are a projection of consciousness power and activity. By cultivating this recognition again and again, understanding arises and mental phenomena begin to subside of their own accord. Stability in perpetual recognition gives radical freedom.

You must learn to sustain recognition. Liberation and freedom is the experience of nondual realization. When at rest, there is no motion of mind and there can be an unadorned perception unclouded with residues of delusion and dichotomies. When you look directly at your own awareness there is nothing to be seen. This is objectless introversion; there is nothing specific to be perceived. Nonetheless, this recognition is not an absence, but the perfect secret fullness. After this recognition you must also recognize mental movements and projections before they become the chains of attachment and aversion. You have to learn to detach from wildly running concepts and dualistic cognitive processes before they turn into those chains of confinement. This is what mind can do to the unvigilant. The mind is like a drunken artist and all beings under the influence of such a mind are subject to entanglement in its seductions and the pictures it draws in the passive thought processes.

Pure Gnosis is the ground of all being. Without getting habituated in formal meditative sessions and structured practices, stay in constant wholetime contemplation. Sustain your recognition all the time. Spontaneous reflexive recognition of the flow of mental factors as they appear and disappear,

73

without any preference or prejudice, makes them all weaken and vanish. Then there is again the recognition of the absence of the thought processes of mind, which puts you back in your primordial essence. By virtue of a new habit, habitual reflexive recognition of mental motions and projections as contractions of the energies of pure consciousness, you can relax in a knowing equanimity. Thoughts are like waves on an ocean, but no matter how large or long the tumbling wave, it remains in and as the ocean. Quiescent mind is in the state of Gnosis, so stay relaxed. If mind is active, just let it be so, and whatever wave comes tumbling by is recognized as the natural expression of Gnosis itself. So in this you can stay relaxed. Recognize like this again and again, and yet again relax.

Become established in the nature of your original existential condition. Cut through the knots of attachment and aversion and all dichotomized opinion. When the mind is free of all ego-motivated ambition and all belief supports, that is correct vision and the proper way to abide. Judgmental thought may come but it is an old web of habit to avoid getting entangled in, so stay present in holistic lucidity, responsive and not reactive, flexible in unobstructed freedom. You cannot perceive non-conceptual truth with a structured intellect, so remain in contemplative relaxation, real Gnosis free of dualistic projections and subtle compulsive delusions.

This is a direct experience of primordial consciousness. This induces a quiescent state of mind that breaks the vicious circle of moral and mental cause and effect. Formless contemplation deconditions consciousness. Formless contemplation does not use concentration on any objective form, but is intent on discovering that primordial consciousness that is able to perceive all forms, all sense impressions, and all thoughts. Formless contemplation consists of just letting the original existential condition prevail spontaneously, moment by moment; this existential condition is actually conditionless, the state of precausal primal awareness.

This is the correct and most profound approach, and while learning to do this formless contemplation, a question arises as to how to sustain such pure perception, the fundamental awareness of holistic unity unclouded by thought, emotion, or external distractions. This primal awareness is the starting point and also the goal. The practice of maintaining constant vigilance in this lucidity is the essential discipline. Sustaining constant primal unmodified awareness inherent in each moment of perception until gnostic vision arises is the way to transcend all vicious circles of cyclic conflict. This Gnosis becomes the irrevocable norm. So the answer to the question of how to sustain such pure perception will be found by you when you practice again and again and again relax.

You must practice detachment from all conceptual activity. The path to perfect non-attachment is the path to that perfect holistic integral balance wherein your human potential for power and knowledge and will through perfect awareness is maximized. Thoughts do not have to be and should not be suppressed; just let them be and don't follow along with them or pay them much regard. This is a formless contemplation, no object on which to concentrate, no constructed visualization on which to focus, no particular idea to stick to, and no absolute distinction made between subject cognizer and sensory object. All is known as just one functioning. This contemplation is the active expression of gnostic awareness, outside the realm of cause and effect, yet the inherent essence of all subject-object relation. Whatever comes about appears spontaneously without anything separately specific coming to be or ceasing to be, and the awareness from which all is inseparable is likewise the true condition of all conditions. Thoughts and emotions do not need to be purified because they are a function of the continuum of the reality matrix. All thought and emotion are consequences of previous mind function, so if those are negatively oriented and disharmonious they must be altered at their source, which is the mind in its ignorance and wrong views. There is really nothing else to be done; it is enough to leave the mind as it is, with a relaxed presence, not entangled within its displays. Thoughts will dissolve of themselves when the desire in them is not supported. Relax the body and mind and look directly at the mind's functioning and stay free from all tension. Turn your attention to who it is who is the watcher of mental functioning, what it is that recognizes the thought movements. Do this again and again in short sessions throughout each day. This is the most direct of all yogic, meditative, or contemplative pathways to lucid awareness, and the essence of the mystic perennial wisdom.

The entire universe has just one foundation which is unconditioned – an unutterable, self-originating, limitless expanse of potentiality. All beings who remain ignorant of it will continue to wander in the clutch of bewilderment and conflict. Knowledge of the fundamental source is the only way to release yourself from progressive conditioning sustained by the ignorance that accompanies each moment of perception. A ceaseless, unmindful, distorted cognition, and the powers of distraction sustain the error of dualistic discrimination, the basis of all delusion. What is needed is the spontaneous and continual gnostic lucidity that heals the disease (dis-ease) of dualistic perception. Unifying right knowledge and right view, through ratiocination, into pellucid clarity, bring your awareness to such a clarity that the mind submits and enters silence. But silence is no result of any technique of concentration or contemplation. Could silence, the silence of one grounded in the reality of totality, be a result of that understanding? Silence can never be a practice, or effect, that results from understanding anything; silence is equivalent with wisdom and only silence can come close to the expression of what is inconceivable. Since the inconceivable cannot be objectively expressed, silence is so equated with it. Silence is neither a cause nor is it a result of any ideal or any practice or method.

Automaton reactivity can be subjugated and dissolved away, little by little, through the conscientious alteration of speech. Instead of immediately speaking forth as the effect of a previous or ongoing thought-stream, take a deep breath. This extra space between a thought and the spoken words interrupts the mechanical reactivity of the mental processes. You then and there become more intelligently responsive instead of mechanistically reactive. This meditative practice is potent and serves to eliminate coarse reactivity by introducing more vigilance in skillful mindfulness. This is an intelligent use of silence, which is the background of all thought and speech, in order to create a gap of stillness in which things can be re-cognized as-they-really-are, before automatically speaking out a thought. In most cases a thought will be expressed differently after a short meditative gap of silent non-reactivity has been purposefully created. This is a proper tactical use of active attention.

When you are not absorbed in the remembrance of the past or in the imaginations for the future you are outside the illusions of conceptual time and in the unimpeded state of present lucidity. So relax in the way of looking at the thoughts the mind is presently producing. Whatever you notice at this time are only the displays of mental functions reflected in consciousness. But, keep recognizing that consciousness itself does not change according to the changing external scenes and internal thoughts, just as space does not change and is not affected by the objects moving in it. Consciousness itself has no form but is able to manifest all forms. The real nature of all is the one foundational essence – consciousness – beyond all phenomena and mental constructs yet immanent in them. Confusion comes from not realizing this. Many times during each day reflect on this truth and remember your own essence, stay disengaged and detached but vigilantly receptive and open. In the gap between the intermittent flow of your thoughts is the clear wakefulness of thought-free lucidity, so stay relaxed and easy in the absence of mental fixations. Don't fixate on anything, even non–fixatedness. Your lucid awareness is not confined in any way. Just remain in a witnessing awareness. Knowing the truth, undistracted, in vigilant attentiveness, the mind will do nothing because your attention is acutely active. If thoughts arise, don't try to modify the mind by trying to suppress it or improve it; don't try to confine your attention to any kind of object or activity. Just relax in attentive vigilance and know yourself as lucid awareness.

This contemplation is not an escape from or an obliviousness toward anything; it is a radiant and vibrant quality of cognition, a clear and intelligent state of awareness where everything is recognized and known spontaneously as an aspect of functional totality; you don't have to think about it. Consciousness is like a clear mirror, a deep reflective ocean with a perfectly calm and lucid surface that can reflect everything everywhere all simultaneously and perfectly. The reflections here do not influence or change the mirror, so the mirror knows it has no inherent preference or prejudice toward the reflections. This is the training in steady sharpness and stability. Your attention should not stray; don't let your attention get caught or bound up on anything particular. Distractions are just a flow of causal functionality and should not bind up your awareness, just like objects cannot bind up open space. Your awareness is like space in that it has no objective reference point of its own. Look for the beginnings of the contractions of attention which create mind and be alert to this potentiality. Non-alertness will allow this potential to strengthen and manifest the passivity that then allows attraction to or repulsion from distractive events. So just relax attention and be on guard for it to drift, and recognize it as starting to drift when it does so. Maintain stable recognition of yourself as lucid awareness and your mind will stop running toward distractions. Such recognitions are lucid Gnosis.

When everything is experienced as pure already there is no need to continue to react based on egoistic motivations. The reality is that everything is as it should be, according to the laws of relativity. Mind contractions are generally automated fabrications, so don't get absorbed in the delusions of them; just stay in the unfabricated state. If the occasion arises where it would be skillful and beneficial to use the mind, the developed power of ratiocination ensures efficient and powerful capacities for thinking. The spontaneous continuity of presence, the un-binding of the activities of binding, can be known in your own being. Freedom from the influence of mental constructs is the freeing of attention, the de-programming of constrictive habits. This is the entry into the heart of existence, the ever-free, ever-awakened self-knowing Gnosis. Lack of this understanding is the only real defilement to be overcome. Pure knowing experience comes about by letting everything be in its reality as-it-really-is – not as it might be presumed to be. There is no need to add or substantially alter anything. Even so-called defilements do not need to be purified, for they are already perfect defilements. Just recognize them for what they really are and they disappear as

81

presumptions created by mind, resolved by themselves back into their source. This is seeing with the eye of purity.

Be open, aware, and receptive, beyond entanglement in concepts, devoid of fabrications, daydream, and other mental constructs. Your primordial, unconditioned essential being is radiant and allows everything to appear like reflections on a mirror while also retaining the capacity to recognize the absence of duality. Habitual tendencies are then relinquished, ignorance and wrong views vanish away, and wisdom abides without the need for thought structures and conceptualization. The root of all conflict is cut by just recognizing and becoming stable in your essential base consciousness. The mind of such a contemplative is unbound and all becomes a possibility. There is not a point where anyone can remember being unconfined by rules, regulations, laws, assumptions, bewilderments, or effects generated by previous actions and thinking, so at first the prospect of such unbound freedom may be somewhat disquieting or seemingly incredible. One who is stable in this kind of lucidity, however, has no doubts whatsoever and has transcended such limitations. Utter freedom in an expanse like space is the real liberation and is possible because your mind – and everything else – is finally recognized as pure function, perfectly pure already. There is a great oneness and such a discovery permits spontaneity in action and intelligent responsiveness. This wisdom is present even within thoughts and the thinking process and is therefore radiant.

The emergence of individuated holistic intelligence occurs in this manner: one must deliberately and attentively leave the mind in an undisturbed and relaxed condition stabilized in transcendent poise. Re-established many, many times over a long period of time and repetitiously restabilizing the mind and attention in this manner, a quality of open receptivity becomes more and more steady, beyond all distractions and fixations. One then abides naturally in free consciousness as a mere onlooker, a knowing witness of objects and events, coarse and subtle, without any presumption, supposition, superimposition, preference, prejudice, acceptance, or rejection. This perfect contemplative stance is a simple and pure introspective introversion of attention. Doing so diverts the creative energies of consciousness away from its fragmentations and differentiations which are the effects of the mental-sets created through the passivity of attention.

Active subjective introversion of attention is pure contemplative exercise which eventually can become constant holistic awareness. It is the skillful application of active attention in free watchfulness toward the potential to enter into distraction, or to relapse again into passive attention. This is direct contemplative attentiveness focused on the processes of conditioned passive reactivity, mechanistic automatism, and becoming once again free from it. In this way, attention should be actively and deliberately directed toward the potential movements of attention itself. Attention becomes attentive to its own movements, and thus intelligence arises. Intelligence is the pure quality of lucid awareness and in this condition the individual can become fully integrated with the whole of existence, a great knower of truth, a manifest representative of perfect holistic intelligence. This is the sign of Gnosis.

The presence of lucidity is Gnosis. Gnosis is immediate knowing, not dependent on psychosomatic senses, sensorial impressions, perceptions, or accumulated mundane knowledge, an understanding not attained through or dependent upon conceptualization processes. Gnosis is wisdom that can make intelligent use of conceptual knowledge but is not confined by it or bound to any supposition generated by it. The presence of lucidity is the next stage of progress for the consciously evolving individual. It culminates in Gnosis.

ABANDON ATTACHMENT TO RISING THOUGHTS.
THEY WILL THEN SUBSIDE BACK INTO THEIR SOURCE.
RECOGNIZE THE SILENT GAP BETWEEN THOUGHTS.
SUSTAIN ATTENTIVE PRESENCE IN THE GAP.
FLEXIBLE IN UNOBSTRUCTED FREEDOM,
RELAX INTO WHOLETIME LUCID GNOSIS.

The End

Also by this author:

Heart Blossoms

*A Commentary and Analysis of the
Exalted Mahayana Sutra on the
Profound Perfection of Wisdom
Called the Heart Sutra*